Worship BAND PLAY-ALONG

DRUMSET EDITION **Volume 2**

Here I Am to Worship

D1479394

T4-BCO-230

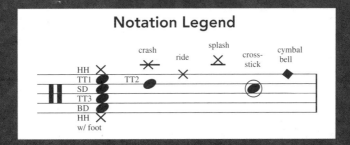

Notation Legend

Recorded and produced by Jim Reith at BeatHouse Music, Milwaukee, WI

Lead Vocals by Tonia Emrich and Jim Reith
Background Vocals by Jim Reith, Janna Wolf and Joy Palisoc Bach
Guitars by Mike DeRose and Joe Gorman
Bass by Chris Kringel
Keyboard by Kurt Cowling
Drums by Del Bennett

ISBN 978-1-4234-1720-0

HAL•LEONARD® CORPORATION

7777 W. BLUEMOUND RD. P.O.BOX 13819 MILWAUKEE, WI 53213

Visit Hal Leonard Online at
www.halleonard.com

Come, Now Is the Time to Worship

Words and Music by Brian Doerksen

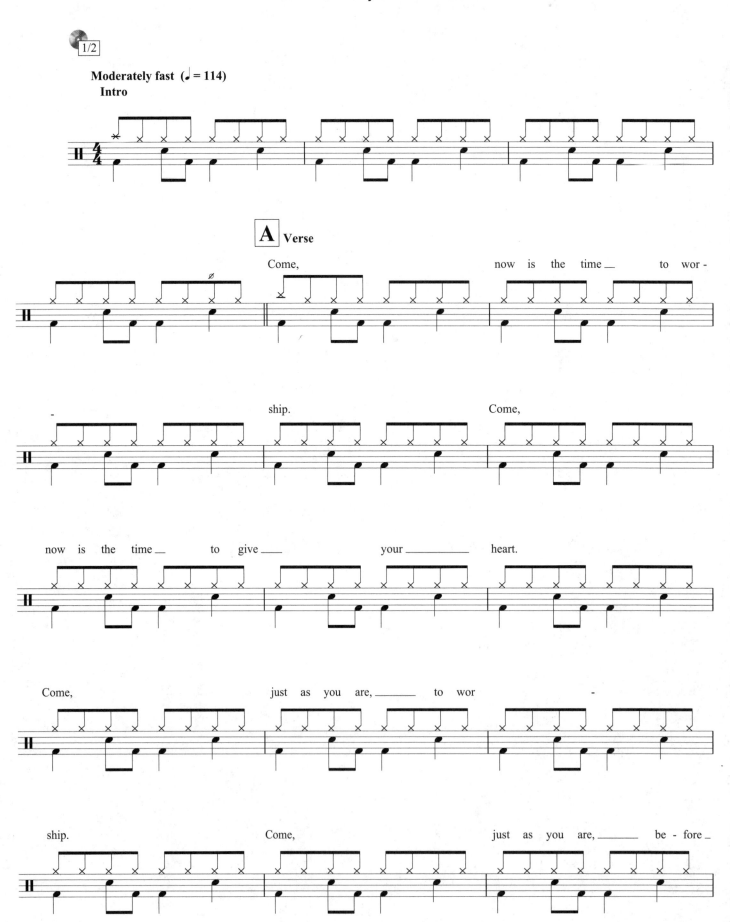

4

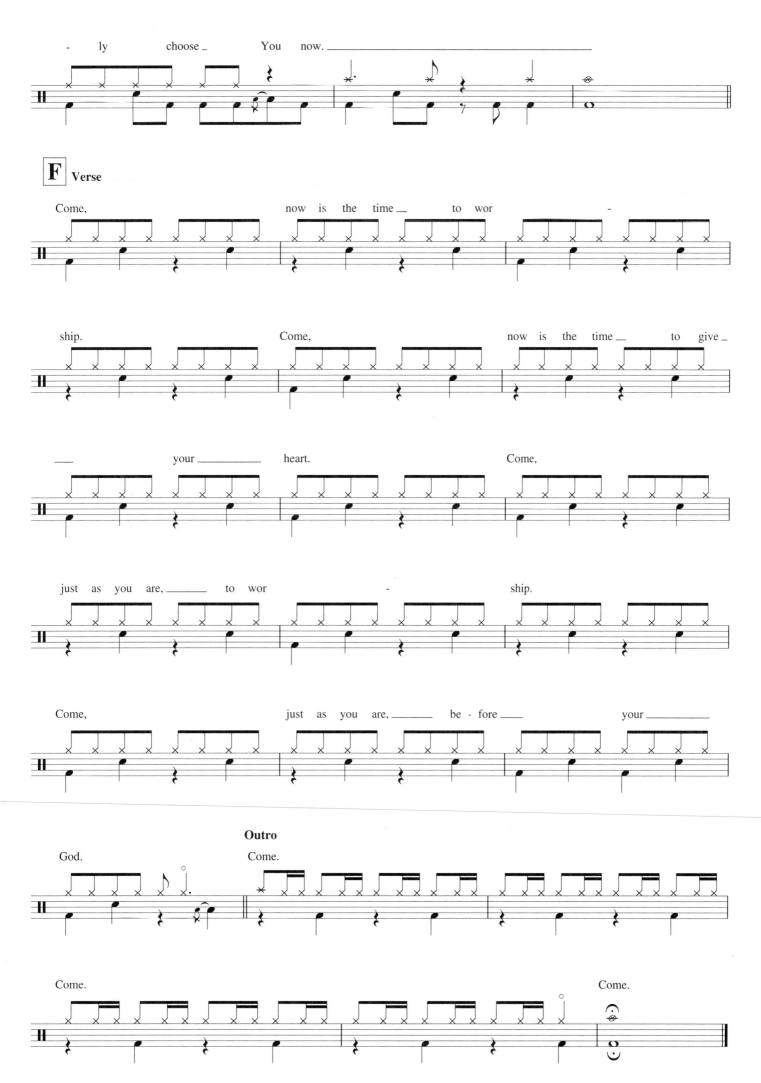

- ly   choose _   You   now. _____

F Verse

Come,   now is the time _   to wor   -

ship.   Come,   now is the time _   to give _

___   your _____   heart.   Come,

just as you are, _____   to wor   -   ship.

Come,   just as you are, _____   be - fore _____   your _____

Outro

God.   Come.

Come.   Come.

5

Give Us Clean Hands

Words and Music by Charlie Hall

lift our souls _ to an - oth - er. And God, let us be _ a gen - er - a - tion that seeks, _

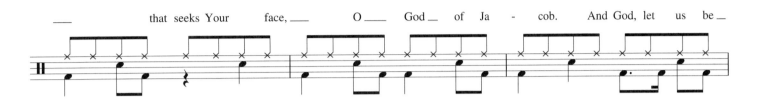

_ that seeks Your face, _ O _ God _ of Ja - cob. And God, let us be _

_ a gen - er - a - tion that seeks, _ that seeks Your face, _ O _ God _ of Ja -

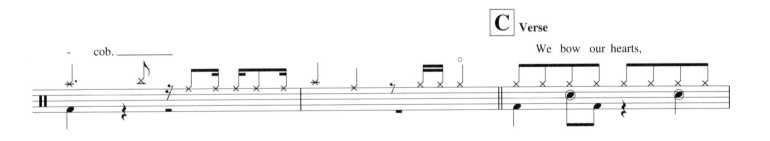

- cob. _____

C Verse

We bow our hearts,

we bend our knees. O Spir - it, come make us hum - ble.

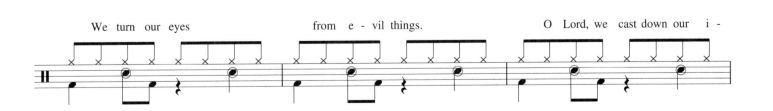

We turn our eyes from e - vil things. O Lord, we cast down our i -

Here I Am to Worship

Words and Music by Tim Hughes

Hear Our Praises

Words and Music by Reuben Morgan

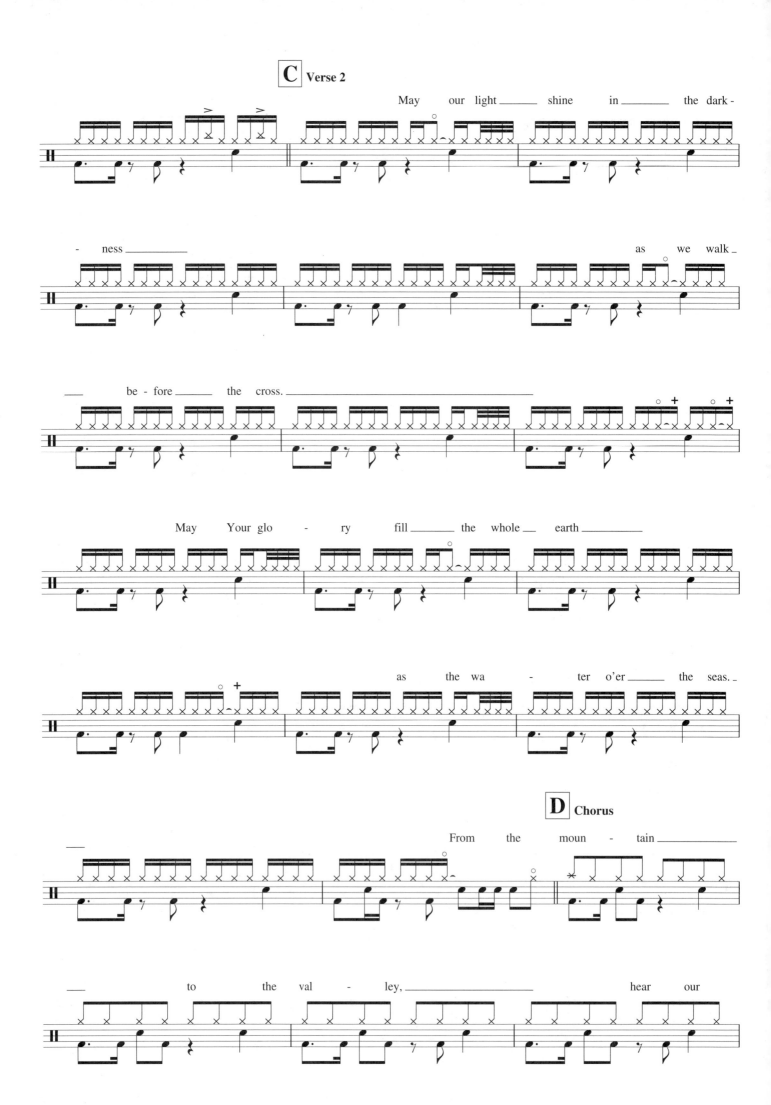

sing - ing _____ fill the air. _____

G **Chorus**

From the moun - tain _____ to the

val - ley, _____ hear our prais - es _____

rise to You. _____ From the

heav - ens _____ to the na - tions, _____

hear the sing - ing _____ fill the

Outro

air. _____

rit.

I Give You My Heart

Words and Music by Reuben Morgan

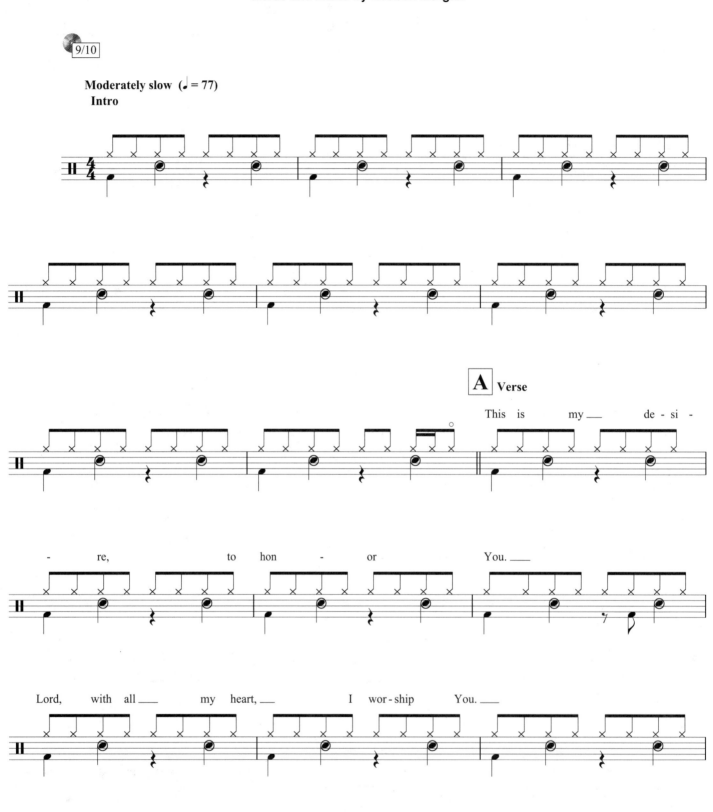

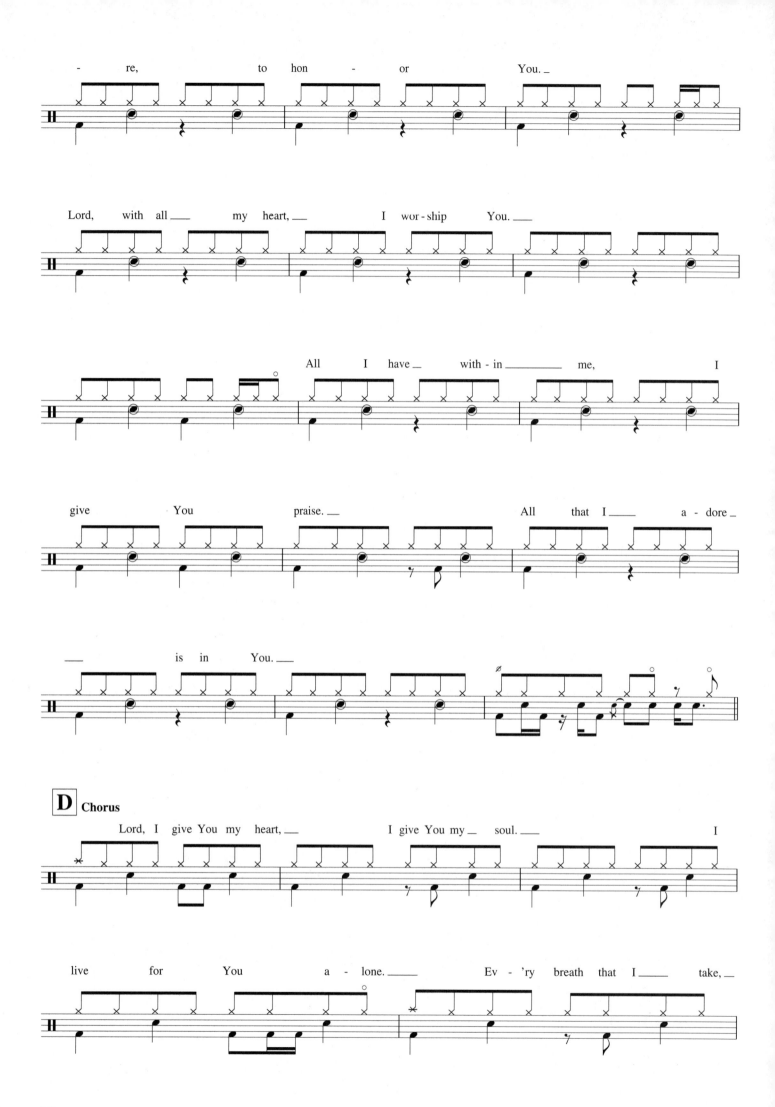

Let Everything That Has Breath

Words and Music by Matt Redman

E Verse 2

F Pre-Chorus 2

You're Worthy of My Praise

Words and Music by David Ruis

Moderately fast (♩ = 110)
Intro

A **Verse 1**

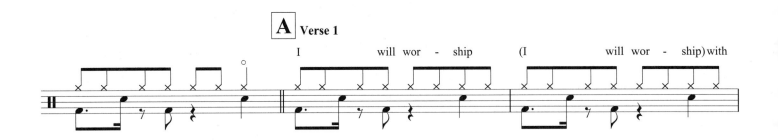

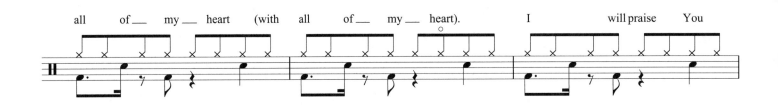

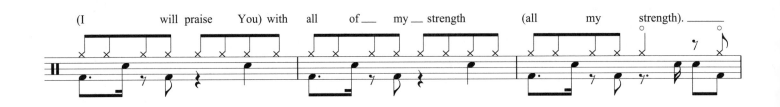

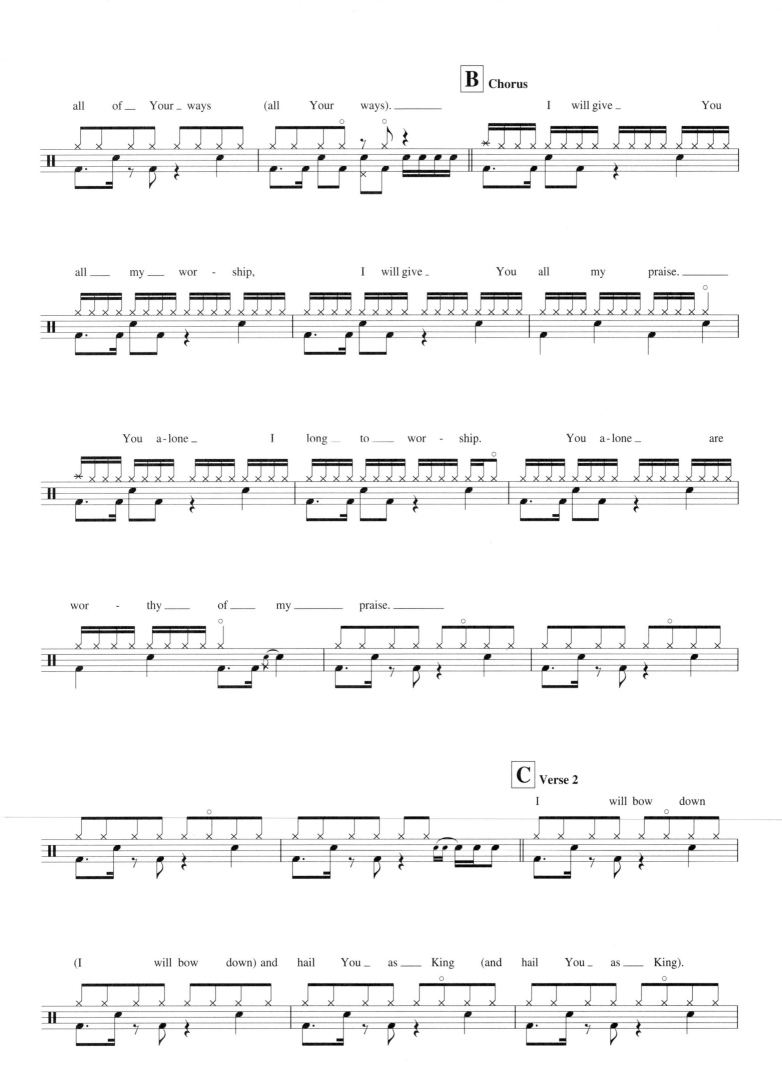

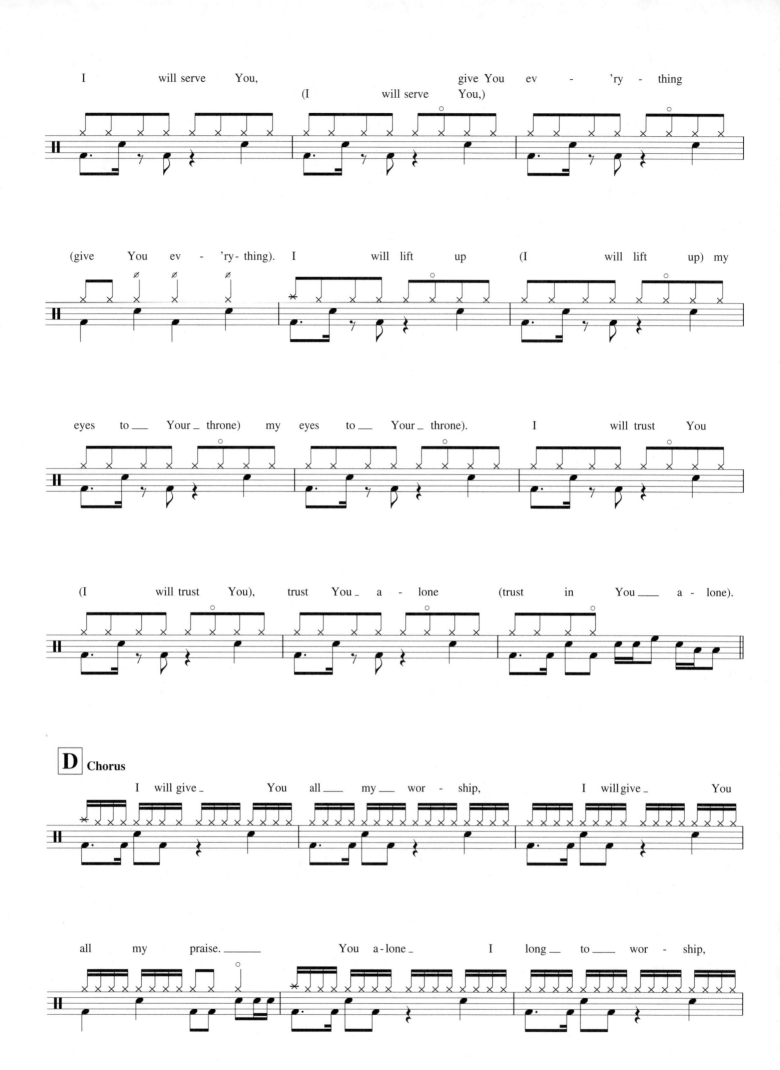

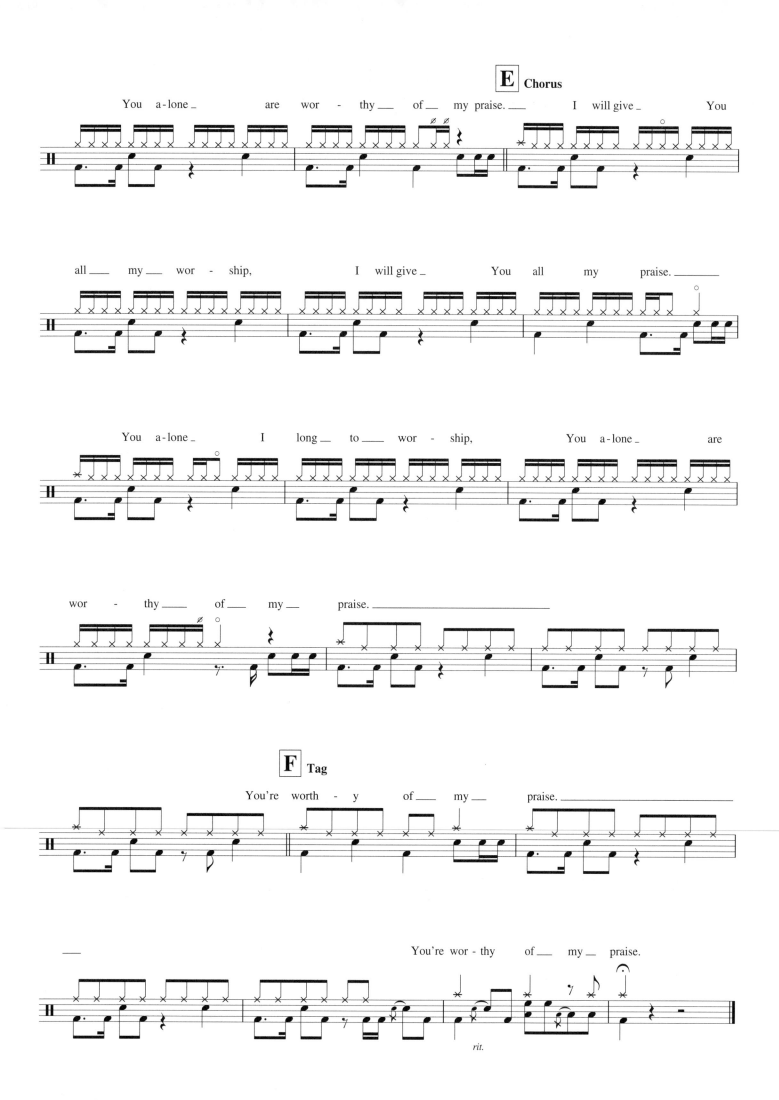

You Alone

Words and Music by Jack Parker and David Crowder

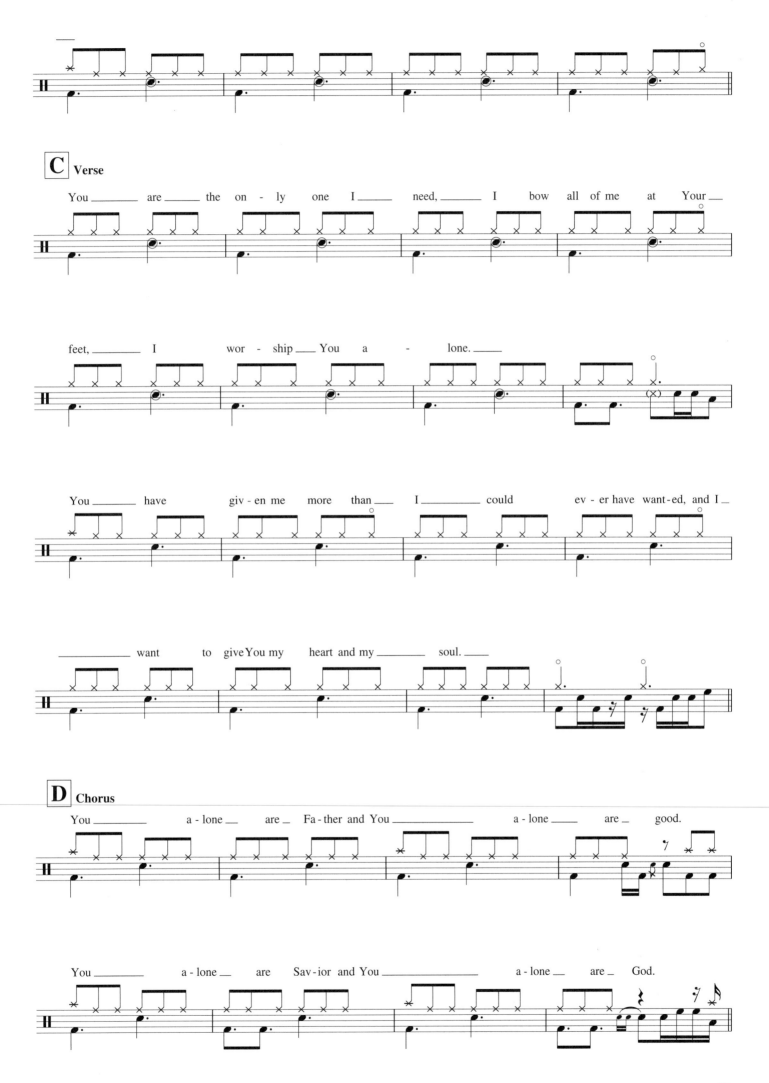

C Verse

You _____ are _____ the on - ly one I _____ need, _____ I bow all of me at Your _____

feet, _____ I _____ wor - ship _____ You a - lone. _____

You _____ have _____ giv - en me more than _____ I _____ could _____ ev - er have want-ed, and I _____

_____ want to give You my heart and my _____ soul. _____

D Chorus

You _____ a - lone _____ are _ Fa - ther and You _____ a - lone _____ are _ good.

You _____ a - lone _____ are Sav - ior and You _____ a - lone _____ are _ God.

slight rit.

COME, NOW IS THE TIME TO WORSHIP

BRIAN DOERKSEN

Key of **D Major**, 4/4

INTRO:

D   G/D D   G/D

VERSE:

D   G/D   D
Come, now is the time to wor   -   ship

A   Em7   D/F♯   G
Come, now is the time to give   your   heart

D   G/D   D
Come, just as you are, to wor   -   ship

A   Em7 D/F♯   G
Come, just as you are, before   your   God

D
Come

CHORUS:

G   D
One day ev'ry tongue will confess You are God

G   D
One day ev'ry knee will bow

G   Bm
Still, the greatest treasure remains for those

      Em7   Asus   A
Who gladly choose You now

(REPEAT VERSE)

(REPEAT CHORUS 2X)

(REPEAT VERSE)

OUTRO:

   D   G/D D   G/D   D (hold)
(Come)   Come   Come

GIVE US CLEAN HANDS

CHARLIE HALL

Key of **G Major, 4/4**

INTRO:

G   D   G/B C   G

VERSE:

G   D   G/B
   We bow our hearts, we bend our knees
C   G
   O Spirit, come make us humble
G   D   G/B
   We turn our eyes from evil things
C
   O Lord, we cast down our idols

CHORUS:

C/D   G   D
Give us clean hands, give us pure hearts
     Em   D   G
Let us not lift our souls to another
          G   D
Give us clean hands, give us pure hearts
     Em   D   G
Let us not lift our souls to another
           G   D
And God, let us be a generation that seeks
        Em   D   G
That seeks Your face, O God of Jacob
           G   D
And God, let us be a generation that seeks
        Em   D   Csus2 (2 bars)
That seeks Your face, O God of Jacob

(REPEAT VERSE & CHORUS)

TAG:

G   D   G/B
   We bow our hearts, we bend our knees
C   G (hold)
   O Spirit, come make us humble

HEAR OUR PRAISES

REUBEN MORGAN

Key of **C Major**, **4/4**

INTRO:

C   Csus   C   Csus

VERSE 1:

C   Csus   C   G/B
    May our homes be filled with dancing

Am   F   Gsus   G
    May our streets be filled with joy

C   Csus   C   G/B
    May injustice bow to Jesus

Am   F   Gsus   G
    As the people turn to pray

CHORUS:

         C   G/B   F/A
From the mountain   to the valley

       Am   Em7   F   Gsus
Hear our praises   rise to You

         C   G/B   F/A
From the heavens   to the nations

       Am   Em7   F   Gsus
Hear the singing   fill the air

(REPEAT INTRO)

VERSE 2:

C   Csus   C   G/B
    May our light shine in the darkness

Am   F   Gsus   G
    As we walk before the cross

C   Csus   C   G/B
    May Your glory fill the whole earth

Am   F   Gsus   G
    As the water o'er the seas

(REPEAT CHORUS)

TRANSITION TO BRIDGE:

C (2 bars)

BRIDGE (2X):

       F   Dm7   Am   Em7
Hallelujah,   hallelujah

       F   Dm7   Gsus   G
Hallelujah,   hallelujah

(REPEAT CHORUS 2X)

OUTRO:

C   Csus   C   Csus   C (hold)

HERE I AM TO WORSHIP

TIM HUGHES

Key of **D Major, 4/4**

INTRO:

D   A   Em7   D   A   G

VERSE 1:

D   A   Em7
Light of the world, You stepped down into darkness

D   A   G
Opened my eyes, let me see

D   A   Em7
Beauty that made this heart adore You

D   A   G (2 bars)
Hope of a life spent with You

CHORUS:

                  D   A
Here I am to worship, here I am to bow down

            D/F♯   G
Here I am to say that You're my God

               D   A
You're altogether lovely, altogether worthy

            D/F♯   G
Altogether wonderful to me

VERSE 2:

D   A   Em7
King of all days, oh, so highly exalted

D   A   G
Glorious in heaven above

D   A   Em7
Humbly You came to the earth You created

D   A   G (1 bar)
All for love's sake became poor

(REPEAT CHORUS)

BRIDGE (2X):

        A/C♯   D/F♯   G
And I'll never know   how much it cost

    A/C♯   D/F♯   G
To see my sin   upon that cross

(REPEAT CHORUS 2X)

TAG:

D   A   Em7
Light of the world, You stepped down into darkness

D   A   G (hold)
Opened my eyes, let me see

I GIVE YOU MY HEART

REUBEN MORGAN

Key of **D Major, 4/4**

INTRO:

Gmaj7   A/G   F♯m7   Bm7

Gmaj7   A/G   F♯m7   G/A

VERSE:

D   A/C♯ Bm7
This is my de - sire

    G   D   A
To hon - or You

Bm7   A/C♯   D
Lord, with all   my   heart

        Cmaj7   G   A
I worship You

D   A/C♯ Bm7
All I have with - in me

  G   D   A
I give You praise

Bm7   A/C♯   D
All that I a - dore

    Cmaj7   G   A
Is in You

CHORUS:

D   A
Lord, I give You my heart

              Em7
I give You my soul

 G/A
I live for You alone

D   A/C♯
Ev'ry breath that I take

              Em7
Ev'ry moment I'm awake

   G/A   (**Gmaj7   A/G   G/A**)
Lord, have Your way in me

(REPEAT VERSE)

(REPEAT CHORUS 2X)

OUTRO:

Gmaj7   A/G   F♯m7   Bm7

Gmaj7   A/G   F♯m7   G/A   D (hold)

LET EVERYTHING THAT HAS BREATH

MATT REDMAN

Key of **E Major, 4/4**

INTRO:

E5   E5/D♯   C♯m7   Asus2 A/B

E5   E5/D♯   C♯m7   Asus2 A/B   F♯m7 (2 bars)

CHORUS:

E5   E5/D♯
Let everything that, everything that

C♯m7   Asus2   A/B
Everything that has breath praise the Lord

E5   E5/D♯
Let everything that, everything that

C♯m7   Asus2   A/B   F♯m7 (2 bars)
Everything that has breath praise the Lord

VERSE 1:

E5
Praise You in the morning

E5/D♯
Praise You in the evening

C♯m7   Asus2
Praise You when I'm young and when I'm old

E5
Praise You when I'm laughing

E5/D♯
Praise You when I'm grieving

C♯m7   Asus2
Praise You ev'ry season of the soul

PRE-CHORUS 1:

 F♯m7   E/G♯
If we could see how much You're worth

     F♯m7   E/G♯
Your pow'r, Your might, Your endless love

     F♯m7   E/G♯   A   A/B
Then surely we would never cease to praise

(REPEAT CHORUS)

VERSE 2:

E5
Praise You in the heavens

E5/D♯
Joining with the angels

C♯m7   Asus2
Praising You forever and a day

E5
Praise You on the earth now

E5/D♯
Joining with creation

C♯m7   Asus2
Calling all the nations to Your praise

PRE-CHORUS 2:

 F♯m7   E/G♯
If they could see how much You're worth

     F♯m7   E/G♯
Your pow'r, Your might, Your endless love

     F♯m7   E/G♯   A   A/B
Then surely they would never cease to praise

(REPEAT CHORUS 3X)

END ON E

YOU ALONE

JACK PARKER and DAVID CROWDER

Key of **E Major, 6/8**

INTRO:

E E/G# Asus2

E E/G# Asus2

VERSE:

E E/G# Asus2
You are the only one I

E E/G# Asus2
Need, I bow all of me at Your

E E/G# Asus2 E E/G# Asus2
Feet, I worship You alone

E E/G# Asus2
You have given me more than

E E/G# Asus2
I could ever have wanted, and

E E/G# Asus2 E E/G# Asus2
I want to give You my heart and my soul

CHORUS:

E E/G# Asus2
You alone are Father

E E/G# Asus2 B
And You alone are good

E E/G# Asus2
You alone are Savior

E E/G# Asus2 (B)
And You alone are God

INTERLUDE:

E E/G# Asus2

E E/G# Asus2

(REPEAT VERSE & CHORUS)

BRIDGE:

E E/G# Asus2
I'm alive, I'm alive, I'm alive, I'm alive

E E/G# Asus2
I'm alive, I'm alive, I'm alive, I'm alive

E E/G# Asus2
I'm alive, I'm alive, I'm alive, I'm alive

E E/G# Asus2 B
I'm alive, I'm alive

(REPEAT CHORUS 2X)

OUTRO:

E E/G# Asus2

E E/G# Asus2 E (hold)

YOU'RE WORTHY OF MY PRAISE

DAVID RUIS

Key of **E Major**, 4/4

INTRO:

E   D/E

VERSE 1:

E   *Echo:*
I will worship (*I will worship*)

    D/E
With all of my heart (*with all of my heart*)

A
I will praise You (*I will praise You*)

       E   F♯m7   Bsus B
With all of my strength (*all my strength*)

E
I will seek You (*I will seek You*)

D/E
All of my days (*all of my days*)

A
I will follow (*I will follow*)

E   F♯m7   Bsus B
All of Your ways (*all Your ways*)

CHORUS:

E   B
I will give You all my worship

F♯m7   A   Bsus B
I will give You all my praise

E   B
You alone I long to worship

F♯m7   A   Bsus B   E   D/E
You alone are worthy of   my praise

VERSE 2:

E
I will bow down (*I will bow down*)

    D/E
And hail You as King (*and hail You as King*)

A
I will serve You (*I will serve You*)

         E   F♯m7   Bsus B
Give You ev'rything (*give You ev'rything*)

E
I will lift up (*I will lift up*)

    D/E
My eyes to Your throne (*my eyes to Your throne*)

A
I will trust You (*I will trust You*)

E   F♯m7   Bsus B
Trust You alone (*trust in You alone*)

(REPEAT CHORUS 2X)

TAG:

        A   Bsus B   E   D/E
You're worthy of   my praise

        A   Bsus B   E (hold)
You're worthy of   my praise